A Moment in My Life

A Moment in My Life

Summer of 1974

Jesse Ambriz

authorHOUSE®

AuthorHouse™
1663 Liberty Drive
Bloomington, IN 47403
www.authorhouse.com
Phone: 1 (800) 839-8640

© 2015 Jesse Ambriz. All rights reserved.

No part of this book may be reproduced, stored in a retrieval system, or transmitted by any means without the written permission of the author.

Published by AuthorHouse 02/08/2016

ISBN: 978-1-5049-2607-2 (sc)
ISBN: 978-1-5049-7483-7 (hc)
ISBN: 978-1-5049-2608-9 (e)

Print information available on the last page.

Any people depicted in stock imagery provided by Thinkstock are models, and such images are being used for illustrative purposes only. Certain stock imagery © Thinkstock.

This book is printed on acid-free paper.

Because of the dynamic nature of the Internet, any web addresses or links contained in this book may have changed since publication and may no longer be valid. The views expressed in this work are solely those of the author and do not necessarily reflect the views of the publisher, and the publisher hereby disclaims any responsibility for them.

A MOMENT IN MY LIFE SUMMER OF 1974

When it came to giving advice dad was a man of few words. Just like riddle's, we needed to figure out what it was he was trying to make us understand.

One advice which he once gave me, and that I have always kept in my mind was when he said to me "son, god gives us the beginning and the end of life. What happens in between is up to us".

Yes, I figured that one out quickly. My life was all on me, and I was not to depend on no one else, when it came to my future, and my goals.

My name is Marco, and this story is of me, and my older brother Angel growing up as teenagers, and going through some difficult times during the summer of 1974, and it was the same time that a special girl name Sheryl came into my life. Both she and Angel had a great impact in my life.

I will gladly share my story as much, and as closely as I can remember of my life during the summer of 1974.

I was born the third eldest of ten siblings. Mom had seven children with her first marriage, and three more from her second.

We were all born and raised in the worst and roughest neighborhood of a city in Texas. The place was a government housing assistance, and known too many as the Westside barrio.

We lived in a three bedroom unit. One bedroom was shared by all the boys, and another was shared by the girls. And of course mom and dad shared the third bedroom.

The barrio had a bad reputation. It was known for an area of high violent crimes, prostitution, and drug trafficking.

Unless they were call to investigate a problem we would hardly ever see a police cruiser patrolling the neighborhood. And medical emergency personnel would not respond to the area without a police escort.

It seem like the neighborhood had been neglected by not only the elected people in the city government, but also by the neighborhood residents themselves.

The streets and sidewalks needed serious repairs. There were not enough street lights, and the few we had were not working.

Everywhere you went in the neighborhood, you would see dead dogs, and cats lying in the middle of the street, or sidewalks, broken down cars parked in the front yards of many residences, and homeless winos sleeping on the bus benched, or sidewalks.

Yes we lived in deep poverty, and our lives were very hard and difficult growing up through our childhood and teenage years. We were so poor that there were many times I looked forward to going to school, only because it was a sure thing that I would have something to eat for the day. The little food we received from the government assistance program only lasted for about three days, if we were lucky.

I was only about 9 or 10 years old when I started working by selling the newspaper, and the street corner I was assigned to sell the paper was in a very rough part of the neighborhood.

My shift started at about 5:00 a.m., and ended when I finished selling all the papers, which was usually around 2: OO p.m. I was earning about 5 cents for every paper I sold.

On a good day I would make about a dollar fifty to two dollars, five dollars including tips. That wasn't enough for me, so after getting through selling my papers, I would rush home grab my shoe shine box, and hit every bar in the neighborhood, hustling for customers hoping to earn more money.

That's when I met the biggest drug dealer in the neighborhood. He was one of my regular customers, and a big tipper. Only problem was that he, and Angel didn't see eye to eye.

Angel did not want me associating with this drug dealer because he had a bad reputation and he was a bad influence on me. He was also a very dangerous person to be around with.

But I learned a lot from this guy, and he took care of me by having his prostitute girls watch over me when I was out going from bar to bar hustling for shoe shine customers.

This very same guy was also known as the robin hood of the barrio, he gave money to people who came to him for financial assistance.

Years later he was arrested, and sentenced to serve time in the state prison. He was then killed along with several other inmates, when they attempted an escape from the state prison. Sadly a state employee was also killed.

Selling newspapers and shoe shining were my jobs from about 9 years old to 12 years old, and during that time I had quickly learned a lot about life and became very street wise.

It was the beginning of the school year for the years of 1973 – 1974. I was 15 years old, and sent away by mom to the Rio Grande Valley to live with an aunt who was mom's younger sister, and I was to attend my junior year at the high school there.

Mom's reason was because I had already been placed in the juvenile detention center twice. My first time was for being involved in a gang fight in school and I was expelled, and the second time was for truancy, and I was suspended.

Oh, and I forgot to mention that I had also been expelled from two different high schools the previous school year, and both times were for my involvement in gang fights.

But I didn't believe mom was being honest with me. I felted that the only reason she sent me away was because of Angel.

Angel had been in trouble with the law too. The first time, was when he was pan-handling for some money in front of a store and refuse to leave when asked to by the store manager.

What Angel was doing was trying to get enough money to buy some medicine for my tooth ache. He wasn't arrested; he was just brought home by the officer.

Angel was always looking out for me. I remember the time I was in need of some shoes and mom couldn't afford to buy me a new pair, so Angel pawned his favorite guitar, and bought me two pairs.

I even remember that one Christmas morning when we all open up our gifts except for Angel. He didn't get a single gift. I asked mom why she didn't get him one. She said that he told her to spend the money on me and make sure that I got what I had asked for.

I was very close to Angel. He was someone I had always looked up to growing up. I guess you could say that I was his number one fan.

To me he was an angel without wings, or a priest without a congregation. On his spare time he would help the elderly, by running errands for them, or fixing their cars, and he would never charge them a penny.

But to many people who didn't know him well enough, he was mean and evil. If only they would have given themselves a chance to know him better, they would have had a different and better opinion of him.

But Angel was also the leader of the toughest gang in the barrio and which I had been a part of too. We were feared by rival gangs, and the residents in the barrio. I could understand why the rival gangs would fear us, but I couldn't understand why the residents in the barrio did.

We were just the toughest, not the meanest. We weren't going around beating up on innocent people, breaking into residences or cars, using or selling drugs. We were only involved in very serious violent gang rumbles; beating up on members of other gangs. Drug dealers were not left out either. They took their share of beatings from us too.

Beating up on drug dealers was Angel's way of cleaning up the neighborhood, and when it came to the prostitutes, Angel would threaten their customers with violence if they continue doing business with the prostitutes.

Family members of our guys in the gang were also safe in the barrio and they were not to be bullied or mess with if you didn't want problems with Angel's gang.

So I moved to live with mom's younger sister and attended the 1973 and 1974 school year in the Rio Grande Valley area. It was a long boring school year, and I became home sick quickly.

I didn't do so well, and didn't make any friends. My grades weren't any better either. I was informed by the school counselor that I would have to repeat the 11th grade again.

It was by the middle of the school year, when I started to become seriously home sick and had made up my mind to go back home, but I toughed it out, and finished the school year.

Even though I was upset with Angel for not returning my calls, or answering my letters, and believed that he was avoiding me, he was the reason I wanted to go back home. I had missed him so much, and I was dying to go back home just to be around him once again.

A Moment in My Life

It finally came. It was a Friday afternoon, and school was over for the year. My mind was set on telling my aunt that I was ready to go back home.

She was in the kitchen cooking dinner when I decided to approach her and tell her of my decision.

(Aunt): Hey son, dinner will be ready soon.

(Marco): Tia, I've been thinking about it for a while and I want to go back home.

(Aunt): You're crazy, what are you talking about?

(Marco): Yes Tia, and I'm calling mom to tell her.

(Aunt): Marco, you have everything you need here. You can have a chance for a better life.

(Marco): Thanks Tia for everything, but I'm calling mom. I want to go home, and I want to go home tonight.

(Aunt): Well go ahead, but I'm not happy about it, and your mom will be less happy.

It was about 6:00 O'clock in the evening when I called mom to tell her of my decision. "Wow" talking about one flying over the coo-coo's nest. Mom lost it and started shouting at me, telling me that I was making the wrong decision and I needed to stay with my aunt.

Mom rudely hung up on me after giving me a piece of her mind. But I had already made up my mind too, and I wasn't going to spend another night away from home.

(Aunt): Well?

(Marco): She became very upset.

(Aunt): No kidding!

(Marco): Tia!

(Aunt): Well! What did you expect?

(Aunt): I'm sure she misses you, and wants you home, but not now, and for good reasons.

(Marco): What reasons Tia?! If you know tell me.

(Aunt): Because of Angel and his gang. She wants you away from them.

(Marco): Angel is my brother, and he has always looked out for me.

(Aunt): He is also the reason why you have been in trouble with the law.

(Marco): I'm sorry Tia, but I going home tonight, even if I have to hitchhike.

(Aunt): Ok! Damn you're so hardheaded. I'll call your mom, but she won't be happy.

(Marco): Ok, thanks.

(Aunt): And don't expect her to welcome you home with open arms.

(Marco): I know.

We learned that there was a bus leaving at 10:00 p.m. that same night. My aunt drove me to the bus station. We arrived 45 minutes early, so we just waited and talked, mainly about my future.

(Aunt): It's not too late to change your mind.

(Marco): Tia, thank you for everything that you have done for me, but I really want to go home.

(Aunt): Ok, but promise me that you will do your best to succeed in life and stay away from your brother Angel and his gang.

(Marco): I promise, to stay away from the gang, but not from Angel. Tia; He is my brother.

(Aunt): I guess you're right. But you better make your life count. Your mother and I believe in you.

(Marco): Why? Why do you'll put so much pressure on me. What is it about me that you'll see, and I can't?

(Aunt): It's because you're so curious about how and why people succeed, basically you are always asking questions and interested on how the world turns

(Marco): How the world turns?

(Aunt): Just a figure of speech.

(Aunt): How many kids your age go around everyday asking questions about life and nothing else? You're always so curious about life and success.

(Marco): Isn't there something going around about how curiosity killed a cat?

(Aunt): Yes, but not in your case. We believe you can make something good out of your life.

The bus finally arrived. I hugged my aunt, kissed her on her right cheek and thanked her for everything that she had done for me. In return she hugged me and kissed me on my left cheek.

(Aunt): Damn, I'm going to miss you. Be safe and please take control of your life.

(Marco): I will, I promise.

I hopped into the bus and sat myself by a window at the rear of the bus and waved goodbye to my aunt as we drove away for the five or six hour trip back home. "Yep" I was on my way back home and to be with Angel once again.

My dear aunt passed away several years later due to a heart attack.

We had been on the road for about an hour already, when I started to wonder if I had made the right decision going back home. There were many times that I thought to myself that I was better off staying with my aunt, if I wanted a better chance for a better life.

I became very tried as I looked out the window watching cars driving the opposite direction and decided to take a nap, but felled sound asleep instead.

It was 10 minutes till 3:a.m., when I was awoken by the bus driver announcing that we were about 30 minutes away from the downtown bus station.

I sat up, cleared my eyes, and again just stared out the window. We drove by several familiar places where I, Angel and the gang use to hang out at.

One familiar place was the drive-in, where Angel used to sneak us in by hiding us in the trunk of his car, then we drove by the county park, where the gang went to meet and dance with girls at Festivals, and it was the same place where we have had several violent rumbles with several rival gangs, which just made me wonder again if I had made the right decision returning home.

It was 3:40 a.m. when we finally arrived at the bus station. I didn't have enough money for a taxi, and the city buses were not operating yet, and I sure wasn't going to call home. I made the decision to walk home carrying my green duffle bag which only contents were my clothes.

I was just a little after 6:00 a.m., when I finally made it to the neighborhood. I don't know why I was surprise to see that nothing had changed. There were still women on street corners hustling for money in exchange for sex, drug dealers walking up and down the streets looking for their buyers, and homeless wino's sleeping on sidewalks and bus benches, the many dead dogs, and cats on sidewalks and in the middle of the streets, along with broken down cars parked on front lawns. The neighborhood was just so filthy.

I just couldn't understand why the guys who volunteered or were drafted to serve in the Vietnam War would return back to this place, and continued living their life's here.

But who was I to question their decision, when I find myself doing the same thing. Again I questioned my own decision of returning home myself.

I was only about 6 blocks away from home when a police cruiser with two officers pulled up next to me. The driver, officer#1 told me to stop as he and the second officer#2 exited the cruiser. I immediately recognized officer#2. He was known to be very aggressive, heavy handed, and short tampered.

This officer was also known to beat up on people just for the hell of it. Angel had been arrested by this same officer twice already and both times assaulted by him for no reason. But Angel never filed a complaint on this officer, because according to him it was a sissy thing to do.

(Off#1):   Where are you going?

(Marco):   Heading home, why?

(Off#1):   Where are you coming from?

(Marco):   The bus station, why?

(Off#1):   What's in the bag your caring?

(Marco):   Just my clothes.

Officer#1 grabbed the bag off my shoulder and handed it over to officer#2. Officer#2 opened up the bag and dumped all my clothes on the sidewalk separating them by kicking them apart as if he was looking for something illegal.

(Marco):   What are you doing?

I shouted to officer#2.

(Off#1):   Shut up, and give me your name.

I then identified myself.

(Off#2):   What! What is your name?

Again I identified myself.

(Off#2):   Do you have a brother name Angel?

(Marco):   He's my older brother, yes.

A Moment in My Life

(Off#2): Are you the one they call "Tuto"?

"Tuto" was the street name given to me by the gang.

(Marco): Yes.

(Off#1): Who is Angel?

(Off#2): He's the leader of the gang in this neighborhood.

(Off#2): Where did you say you were coming from?

(Marco): The bus station.

(Off#2): What were you doing there?

(Marco): I just returned from attending school in the Rio Grande Valley.

(Off#2): You idiot, you should have stayed there. Your brother and your gang are nothing but trouble and problems.

(Marco): I'm not part of the gang anymore. I'm going to work on making something good out of my life.

(Off#2): Bullshit! You, your brother, and your gang have nowhere to go but prison.

With anger and with force officer#2 then grabbed me by my shirt and slammed me against a building causing the back of my head to hit the wall pretty hard.

He then placed his right forearm on my throat adding pressure and causing pain. He continued holding me against the wall and refusing to release the hold, as I continued repeating myself for him to let me go.

(Marco): Get off me! What have I done?

(Off#2): "You Punk" This is what you're going to get every time I catch you out on the streets.

(Off#1): Let him go. He's learned his lesson.

(Off#2): Did you? Did you learn I'm someone not to mess with?

(Marco): Yea! Let me go!

Officer#2 then removed his forearm from my throat and without warning struck me on my chest with a close fist knocking the air out of me, which dropped me down to my knees.

Officer#1 pulled officer#2 away from me and told him to get back in the cruiser.

Officer#2 then started walking back to the cruiser.

(Off#2): Don't forget what I can do to you! You don't want me messing with you! "Punk"!

(Off#1): Gathered your clothes, and go home. I don't want to see you out on the streets either.

In pain and still on my knee's I looked up at officer#1.

(Off#1): What? Is there something you want to say?

(Marco): How can I become a cop? But a good one, not like you guys.

(Off#1): Don't waste your time. "Idiot"

Officer#1 then hopped into the cruiser and drove away with officer#2.

I have never told anyone not even Angel, but as long as I can remember I've always thought that becoming a cop would be something I'm sure I would enjoy being.

And I never told Angel or anyone else what Officer#2 had done to me, because it was like complaining and a sissy thing to do.

Still in pain, I started to gather all my clothes together and placing them back in the duffle bag again wondering of my decision in returning home.

I finally finished gathering my clothes and gathered myself together too. I then continued the rest of my walk home.

I was now just a block away from home, when I saw Benny sweeping the sidewalk outside the neighborhood store. He was the owner of the store and a very good friend of mine. He always had weekend work for me. His only son Danny was killed in Vietnam, and I had always reminded Benny of him.

(Marco): Benny!

I shouted to him from across the street.

(Benny): Marco! Get over here.

I hurried across the street to him; he immediately placed his arms around me, and welcomes me with a tight hug.

(Marco) Benny, I can't breathe.

(Benny): Why did you come back home for? Are you crazy?

(Marco): I came back for Anita.

Anita was five years older than me and Bennie's only daughter. I use to have a big crush on her. She was away attending a University in another state studying to become an attorney. Last I heard was that she got married and never obtained her degree.

(Marco): I'm just kidding Bennie, I'm just home sick, that's why I came back.

(Benny): To what? There is nothing here for you. You were sent away for a good reason.

(Marco): I know, and I know I'm going to hear it from mom too, once I get home.

(Benny): "Boy" I hope she lets you have it, and knocks some sense into you.

(Marco): How's the hood looking anyways?

(Benny): Its worst and Angel and his gang don't make things any better.

(Marco): What do you mean?

(Benny): They have become more violent and constantly coming in and out of jail.

I couldn't believe what Benny had told me about Angel and the gang. What was happening? Was this all true?

A customer showed up and Benny invited me inside the store and told me to help myself to a cold soda.

I grabbed a soda from the freezer and drank it while staring out the store window as Benny attended to the customer. *I then finish the soda and placed the empty bottle on top of the counter.*

(Marco): Thanks for the soda Benny. I'm heading home. I'll talk to you later.

(Benny): Marco you better continue your education, and damn it! Run away from trouble.

(Marco): I will, I promise.

(Benny): Hey! You stupid kid, remember, "Don't just be recognized, be notice".

"Don't just be recognized, be notice" was a phrase Benny always use to say to me and challenged me to find out what he meant by it.

Several months later close to Christmas, Benny was robbed at gun point and shot.

Angel didn't much care for Benny, but he knew how much Benny had helped and cared for me for many years, so he decided to go around asking questions of the guy responsible for it.

Within days he learned who the guy was and turned him into the police, but not before giving the guy a hell of a good beating.

Benny survived the gunshot wound, and closed down the store. He then moved out of the neighborhood. I never saw or heard from him again.

I finally made it home, and quietly sneaked in through the window of the bedroom, which I shared with my brothers.

I placed my duffle bag in the closet and then woke Angel up as he slept on one of the upper bunk beds.

(Marco): Hey, wake up I'm home, make room for me

After shoving him several times, he finally woke up.

(Marco): I'm home

(Angel): Hey little brother, mom said you were coming home. How did you get home?

(Marco): I walked.

Angel then sat up at the edge of the bed and asked me to hop up and sit by him.

(Angel): Why did you come back? You should have stayed in the valley.

(Marco): Well thanks, I missed you too.

Angel then placed his right arm over my shoulders.

(Angel): Sorry, that's not how I meant it. I missed you too, but mom sent you away for good reasons and I agreed with her.

(Marco): This is my home, and here is where I belong.

(Angel): I love you very much little brother, but you need to go back and stay with our aunt. There is no future for you here. Not even a chance for a better life.

Feeling hurt and not wanting to hear any more of what Angel was telling me, I quickly changed the subject.

(Marco): I ran into Benny on my way home.

(Angel): Yeah.

(Marco): Yeah, he said you and the gang have been getting into trouble with the law.

Angel suddenly, and with anger grabbed a tight hold of my front shirt.

(Angel): Don't concern yourself with what is going on with me and the gang. We are no longer your business.

I then pulled Angel's hands off my shirt.

(Marco): I didn't ask about you or the gang! I only asked about the neighborhood.

(Angel): Ok, I'm sorry, but look there is something about you that makes me believe you can make something good of yourself, so you need to be around positive people.

(Marco): Don't you think you're a positive person?

(Angel): Not for you I'm not.

(Marco): But I have always looked up to you.

(Angel): Don't ever look up to no one, not even me. If you know of someone who has accomplished something good, give them a pad on the back. That should be sufficient enough, but don't admirer or look up to anyone because of their accomplishments.

(Marco): But you always admirer the guys serving in Vietnam.

(Angel): No, I'm only grateful to them.

(Marco): If you don't think you're a positive person for me, does it mean that you are going to stay away from me?

(Angel): Oh god! No you dork. I will always be with you and for you until the end. Now come-on it's still early and I'm still sleepy, let's go to bed. We'll continue our talk later.

(Marco): Can I sleep next to the window?

(Angel): Yeah, I guess.

I tucked myself under the blanket in-between Angel and the window.

(Marco): I really missed you Angel.

(Angel): Yea, yea I missed you too.

(Marco): I love you.

(Angel): Damn little brother, did you go gay while you were away?

(Marco): What!

(Angel): Shhhh, quiet you're going to wake up the others.

(Marco): Well, what did you say?

A Moment in My Life

(Angel): Just kidding, but don't expect me to say I love you too.

Angel then held my left hand tight, and said goodnight.

(Marco): Angel.

(Angel): Now what?

(Marco): Who do we know that is a positive person?

(Angel): Well, You know that guy we call "Mama's Boy".

(Marco): Yea, what about him?

(Angel): Well you remind me of him.

(Marco): What! Now I'm a mama's boy?

(Angel): Shhh, be quiet you dork; you're going to wake up everybody.

(Marco): Well, what do you mean?

(Angel): I mean that guy is going places. He is going to make a name for himself. I see a lot of good in him.

(Marco): Yeah, I believe he is too. So I remind you of him?

(Angel): Yes! Now go to sleep! Talk to you later.

(Marco): Ok, ok goodnight we'll talk later.

(Angel): Hey!

(Marco): What?

(Angel): Yea, I love you too dork. Goodnight.

(Marco): I know that. Goodnight.

That guy we call "Mama's Boy" later became a City Councilmen, then Mayor and later appointed the Secretary of Housing Urban Development by the then President of this country.

It was about 10:00 a.m. when I was awakened by Angel slapping a pillow on my face.

(Angel): Wake-up lazy dork, mom is getting breakfast ready.

I immediately jumped off the bed and rush over to the bathroom to wash up. Twelve in the family with only one bathroom, we would always hurry to be the first one in.

I finished washing up, and walked into the kitchen as mom prepared breakfast. It wasn't much just toast bread, and eggs.

(Marco): Hi mom

(Mom): Hi son, you gained weight.

(Marco): Yea maybe ten pounds more. Are you still upset?

(Mom): Yes I am, but we'll talk about that later. Now go sit down breakfast it ready.

I kissed mom, and told her I loved her, and missed her, then sat myself down at the table.

Dad, Angel, and my older sister Janie were already sitting at the table. The rest of the kids were sitting down in the living room with their trays, and watching Saturday morning cartoons.

Mom finished serving us, and sat down by me. It was very quiet for the first two or three minutes which seemed like an hour.

(Dad): Did your mom tell you that we are very disappointed in you. Do you know how upset we are?

(Marco): I know, but don't worry about me; I'll continue to go to school and graduate.

(Dad): How do we know that for sure? You let us down by returning home.

(Marco): I can make it dad. I know I can, just give me a chance.

(Dad): Chance? Your life is up to you; don't expect people to give you chances if you're not willing to try.

Angel suddenly stood up looked at dad and slammed his hands on the table.

(Angel): Dam it! He just got home, and you are already drilling him. Leave him alone!

(Dad): Don't raise your voice, or use that language in this house.

(Angel): Forget it! I'm out of here! Sorry mom.

Angel then stormed out of the house, without finishing his breakfast.

At first Angel didn't accept dad, when dad first came into our lives. Angel had been the man of the house before mom married dad.

(Dad): We are just concerned. Angel is leading the wrong life, and we don't want you to follow behind him.

(Marco): Don't worry too much about me. I promise that I will continue school, and stay out of trouble.

(Mom): Whether we like it or not, you're back, and all we can do is have faith that you can make it.

(Dad): And don't worry too much about Angel. That's my job. I will always be here for him.

Even though dad wasn't very happy with Angel, and had already given up on him, he always had his hand extended out to him, if only Angel would just swallow his pride.

(Mom): I can see that you're still tried. Finish your breakfast, so you can get back to sleep. It's still early.

(Dad): Your mom, and I, including Angel believe in you. Make us proud.

(Marco): I promise.

I then finish my breakfast, and said my goodnights to everyone, and got myself back to bed.

As I lay in bed, and before falling asleep, I thought about how much mom, dad, and Angel believed in me, and wondered of how I was going to make things right for me.

It was around 8:00 at night, when I woke up, and joined mom in the living room. She was watching one of her favorite western shows call the "Rifle Man".

Dad was at work, and the rest of the kids were outside playing.

(Marco): You still enjoy watching that show?

(Mom): Yes, still my favorite.

(Marco): Did Angel come back?

(Mom): No. Why are you asking?

(Marco): Well he was very upset, when he left this morning.

(Mom): Don't worry, it's nothing new.

Minutes later Angel walked in the house with a smile.

(Angel): Hey little brother, get dress, I'm taking you to say hello to the guys.

(Mom): What! No you're not!

(Angel): Mom, don't worry. We'll be back in an hour.

(Mom): No, he is not leaving this house. It's late already.

(Angel): Mom, I'll watch out for him, we are just going to say our hello's, and come back.

(Marco): Mom I will be okay. I promise to be back quick.

(Mom): Angel, you better take care of him, and return back before your father gets home.

(Angel): We promise.

I quickly got up, hurried to the bedroom, and changed into my best clothes.

(Marco): I'm ready Angel, let's go.

(Angel): We will be home soon mom.

(Mom): Please do not get into any trouble, and get home before your father does.

Both Angel and I kissed mom, and assured her that we would be back before dad return.

(Marco): Where are the guys at?

(Angel): The whole gang is at pool hall waiting on us.

The pool hall was at the only neighborhood ice house where the gang hung out at. The owner didn't mind the gang being there. We made him feel safe.

(Angel): We are not taking the car, we're walking. It's only six blocks away.

(Marco): Ok

We walked pass our neighbor Marisa's house, and saw her sitting outside the front porch smoking a cigarette, and drinking a beer.

(Marisa): Hey Angel is that Tuto with you?

(Marco): Yes it's me Marisa. I'm back.

(Marisa): Yea, I heard you were back. Where are you boys going?

(Angel): We're heading to pool hall.

(Marisa): Bring me back a six pack, and we can party together.

(Angel): In your dreams. Go back inside, and take care of your kids. Are do you even know where they're at?

(Marisa): Shit on you, you punk.

Marisa tossed her cigarette at us and stormed inside the house cursing at Angel.

(Marco): Ga, why did you say that to her?

(Angel): Cause she is still a drunk and doesn't watch over her kids.

Marisa was in her late 20's, and single with three kids.

She was also very pretty, and she also used to be a very popular girl in the neighborhood, and back in her high school days too. She was more popular than the school cheerleaders. They were jealous of her themselves.

But Marisa was also going through some hard times herself. Like everyone else, she struggle to make ends meet, and she did what she had to do to support her family. She fell from grace with many in the neighborhood. She was known as the neighborhood drunk and for sleeping with men for financial support. I have always felt that she had been wrongly judge by the people in the neighborhood.

Years later she met and married a guy who moved her and her kids out of the barrio, and bought them a house. I was very happy for her and her family.

(Marco): I'll race you to the pool hall.

(Angel): Ok, but you need to give me a head start.

(Marco): Is it because I'm too fast for you?

(Angel): No you dork! You're wearing sneakers and I am wearing my Stacy's shoes.

(Marco): Ok, you take off first, and I'll count till five before I start running.

(Angel): Ok, count.

Angel took off running, and after the count of five, I began running too. I caught up to him as we ran pass a man fixing a flat tire.

Angel stopped all of a sudden, and started walking back toward the man fixing the flat.

(Marco): What's wrong? What are you doing?

(Angel): Just follow me.

(Marco): Angel, what are you going to do?

(Angel): I'm not going to do anything. You are.

(Marco): What?

As we walked toward the man I could see that he was an elderly man showing a little fear, and

A Moment in My Life

an elderly lady inside the car was also showing concerned.

The man then started walking backwards away from us, telling us that he did not want any trouble. The poor lady rolled down the window and told us to leave them alone.

(Angel): We are not going to give you any trouble. I just want to help. Give me the tire iron.

The man hesitantly gave Angel the tire iron.

(Angel): Here start fixing the tire for this gentleman.

(Marco): Me? Why me?

(Angel): You didn't expect me to do it wearing my good Stacy's, did you?

(Marco): But I'm wearing my best clothes.

(Angel): Yeah, but you don't look as good in them as I do in my Stacy's. Now hurry up these people need to get to where they're going.

I started changing the tire as Angel and the man smoked a cigarette, and talked about what ever, while I worked on changing the tire. By the time I finished, I was sweaty, dirty, and tired.

I placed the tire iron, the flat tire, and the jack back in the trunk.

(Marco): There I'm finish.

(Angel): What took you so long? It's hot out here, and I'm starting to sweat.

(Marco): Look at me, I'm filthy.

(Angel): Stop it, you're embarrassing me.

The man then shook Angel's hand, and thanked him for his help.

(Marco): What! What about me?

(Angel): Don't tell me you were expecting to get paid?

(Marco): No, but at least a thank you too.

(Angel): Thank you for volunteering little brother. I'm very proud of you.

The man wished Angel well and hoped that Angel's back would get better. He then drove away with his wife.

(Marco): What! What is wrong with your back?

(Angel): Nothing. I just told him that I hurt my back playing ball, and that's why you offered to do all the work.

(Marco): Wow, I don't believe it.

(Angel): Stop crying like a baby. Now let's hurry to the pool hall, before it gets too late you dork.

We finally arrived at the pool hall. The whole gang was there. The place was packed, and I was greeted by everyone with open arms.

As I was saying my hello's to everyone, I notice a very beautiful girl about my age playing at one of the pool tables alone. I then pulled Angel aside from the others.

(Marco): Wow, who is that beautiful girl at the pool table?

(Angel): That is Sheryl, Sharon's little sister. We call her Sherry baby.

(Marco): Wow! She hangs around with you guys?

(Angel): No Sharon just watches after her.

(Marco): She is so beautiful. Does she have a boyfriend?

(Angel): No, but don't waste your time. She has every guy in the hood chasing after her, and she won't even give them the time of day.

(Marco): I can always try.

(Angel): Ok, but don't come crying to me, when she breaks your heart.

I excused myself from the gang and started approaching Sheryl, and as I got closer to her I couldn't help but notice her beautiful big brown eyes and shining long wavy black hair and long eye lashes. She didn't even have any make up on and she sure didn't need it.

(Marco): Hi, my name is Marco.

(Sheryl): ????

(Marco): Angel's younger brother.

(Sheryl): Ok?

(Marco): I heard your name was Sheryl.

(Sheryl): I think it still is?

(Marco): Ok? You mind a game of pool?

(Sheryl): Yes.

(Marco): Great! I'll set up the balls, you go first.

(Sheryl): What are you doing?

(Marco): You did say yes to a game?

(Sheryl): I meant "Yes I do mind playing a game with you".

(Marco): Why?

(Sheryl): Because.

(Marco): You don't say much.

(Sheryl): Nope.

(Marco): Ok, look I just want to play a game and make conversation.

(Sheryl): I'm in no mood for conversations, and I didn't invite you over here.

(Marco): Wow! You spoke more than one word. Now we're getting somewhere.

(Sheryl): We're not getting anywhere, and I would appreciate it if leave me alone, and get back to your friends.

(Marco): My friends? Aren't they your friends too?

(Sheryl): No. I have no choice in being here. My sister Sharon brought me with her.

(Marco): That's right, she is babysitting you.

(Sheryl): She is not babysitting me! I could have stayed home if I wanted too.

(Marco): Wow, you need to see how much prettier you look when you get upset.

(Sheryl): I can get mean too.

(Marco): Really? That would probably make you look gorgeous.

(Sheryl): Look you're wasting your time if you're trying to make friends with me.

(Marco): And I bet it would be the best time I've ever wasted.

Angel then shouted at me reminding me that we had to leave, and get home soon.

(Marco): Well, I got to go now.

(Sheryl): Well go! Run! Fly out of here.

(Marco): Ok, but you need to stop having bi-polar moments.

(Sheryl): Bi-polar? You need to start doing the disappearing act!

(Marco): Ok, ok bye.

(Sheryl): Ok! Bye! Adios!

(Marco): Ok already, but are you purposely getting upset just to look prettier for me?

(Sheryl): Yes! No! I meant just go!

(Marco): Ok, I'm leaving, but first, what time is it?

(Sheryl): Aaahhh Marco, Its ten minutes till ten!

(Marco): Wow! You remembered my name.

(Sheryl): It's only because I will never forget the name of the dummy that showed up full of dirt, and grease on his clothes.

(Marco): Oh that. I helped change a tire on my way over here………

(Sheryl): God! Who cares? Now go!

(Marco): Ok, but let me just say one last thing before I walk away.

(Sheryl): You got to be kidding me! Now what!

(Marco): Angel was wrong. He said that you would never give me the time of day.

(Sheryl): Bye! Go home! Brush your teeth! Say your prayers, and go to bed! Adios! Goodnight! I never met you! And I never saw you!

(Marco): Damn, I love you too.

(Sheryl): What??????!

(Marco): I'm going home, brush my teeth, and say my prayers, go to bed, and dream of you.

(Sheryl): You are crazy!

(Marco): I wasn't before I met you.

(Sheryl): We never met! Bye! We'll talk later!

(Marco): Did you say we'll talk later?

(Sheryl): Damn, Ok! Just go before I change my mind!

(Marco): Ok, goodnight Sherry Baby.

(Sheryl): What?

(Marco): Sherry Baby, isn't that what they call you?

(Sheryl): No, and don't you start calling me that.

(Marco):   Blah, Blah, Blah

(Sheryl):   You're a suborned guy, aren't you?

(Marco):   Not as suborned as you are, plus you have an attitude.

(Sheryl):   It's my attitude, like it or not.

(Marco):   I'll deal with it, I'm sure it would be worth it.

(Sheryl):   What do you mean deal with it? I haven't said for sure that I want to hang with you.

(Marco):   Blah, Blah, Blah

(Sheryl):   Yeah, Blah, Blah whatever that means.

I then walked away, and headed back to the gang to say my goodbyes. I then notice Sheryl looking over toward me. I waved goodbye to her. I was surprise, and happy to see her finally break a smile. Angel, and I left the pool hall, and started heading back home.

(Angel):   Well, how did it go with Sheryl?

(Marco):   She gave me the time of day, something you said she would never do. That's good huh?

(Angel):   She probably felt sorry for you. Don't expect much more from her.

(Marco): How come I never knew of her?

(Angel): Like I'm trying to do with you, Sharon keeps her away from the gang.

(Marco): Well I have a feeling that we are going to be a hit.

(Angel): Don't get your hopes up high.

(Marco): Why?

(Angel): Well, you saw how beautiful she is, beautiful enough to move to Hollywood.

(Marco): Why would she want to move to that little town?

(Angel): You're such a dork! Hollywood California! Not Hollywood Park!

(Marco): Yeah, you're right, she is that beautiful.

Angel, and I started joking around, and throwing rocks at street signs, when he suddenly shouted "Damn it" and picked up a large stick that was lying close by, then started chasing after a guy who was standing at a street corner up ahead.

(Marco): Angel what are you doing?

(Angel): You just wait here!

The guy managed to get away from Angel and I could see that Angel was very upset, when I caught up with him.

(Marco): What was that all about? Who was he?

(Angel): He's a drug dealer, and he sells drugs in the barrio. He is one reason this hood is going down. You know how I feel about drug dealers.

We didn't say much more to each other. I could see how upset Angel was, and he doesn't say much, when he's in his moods.

We made it home before dad did, and said our goodnights to mom. She was relieved to see us home safe.

Angel stayed up watching T.V. in the living room and I went straight to bed. I stared out the window as I listen to the radio and thought of Sheryl before falling asleep.

I woke up about 11:00 a.m., and the first person that came to my mind was of course Sheryl. I just laid there for another fifteen minutes just thinking about how beautiful she was, and if I was ever going to see her again, maybe even have a chance to go on a date with her.

I then got up, and took a quick shower. Angel wasn't home, he had a job as a mechanics helper. Dad was also at work and mom was sitting outside watching the kids playing hide and seek with the other neighborhood kids, so I decided to join her.

(Marco): Hi, mom.

(Mom): Morning son, are you hungry?

(Marco): No, not really.

(Mom): Why don't you go play with the kids?

(Marco): Mom, I'm too old for that.

(Mom): You're only fifteen. Stop growing up too fast.

(Marco): Ok mom, anything that will make you happy, but I'm not going to play hide, and seek with the kids. No way.

(Mom): How did you feel meeting with the guys last night?

(Marco): It was ok.

I then told her about meeting Sheryl.

A Moment in My Life

(Mom): Yes, I know who she is and she is a very pretty girl, but don't let her occupied your mind. You have other things to look forward to.

(Marco): I know.

Mom, and I continued talking mostly about my future, when Nancy who lived down the street walked by caring a bag of groceries.

(Mom): Hi Nancy, good morning.

Nancy looked toward us, and continued walking without saying a word.

(Marco): What's wrong with her? That was rude.

(Mom): Maybe it's what I said.

(Marco): What did you say that was wrong?

(Mom): Angel didn't tell you about Joey.

(Marco): No, what about Joey?

(Mom): He went missing in Vietnam.

(Marco): Wow that explains it.

Joey was Nancy's second youngest. I didn't know much about him except that he was a good singer, and many felt that he had a bright future in singing. Joey was never heard of again.

(Marco): Mom, I want to get me a summer job. I'm going to need school clothes.

(Mom): You're only fifteen, who's going to give you a job? Let me worry about your needs.

(Marco): Well, what am I going to do for the summer?

(Mom): Just enjoy it. Go fishing, swimming, skating, or the movies.

(Marco): Mom, they're not free.

(Mom): One thing at a time son.

(Marco): Ok mom, one thing at a time.

I was still tired, and decided to go back to bed. And since I wasn't allow to hang around with the only friends I had, I did the most I could to occupied myself for the rest of the week.

I helped neighbors with whatever needed to been done around their homes. I try to educate myself by reading books, and once in awhile I did play with the kids, even the hide and seek game.

A Moment in My Life

The following Saturday came around again. It was about 6:00 p.m., when Angel arrived home from work. I was watching Star Trek with two of my younger brothers.

(Angel): Hey little brother, the whole gang is coming over for a get together.

(Marco): Really! Can I hang with you guys?

(Angel): Sure, but you're not going to drink with us. You're only going to sit, and listen.

(Marco): Ok, I can deal with that.

Mom and dad didn't much like the idea of Angel having the guys over, but they rather have him home where he would be safe, and not getting into any trouble.

I was so excited, because I was going to see Sheryl again. It was 9:00 p.m., when everyone finally showed up except Sheryl. I was very disappointed. I guess I can say heartbroken.

So the party went on in the backyard with everyone drinking beer, joking around, dancing, and singing to Mo-town, and disco music.

It was getting close to midnight and the beer was almost all gone.

(Angel): I need some volunteers to go the store, and get us some more beer.

(Joe): I'll go.

(Larry): I'll go too.

(Marco): Can I go with them?

(Angel): Yeah, I guess. Joe and Larry can babysit you. Here's some money get yourself a six pack of soda.

Since Benny had banned Angel and the gang from the store, we decided to walk to another one about seven blocks away.

Larry, and I waited outside the store, while Joe bought the beer. As Joe was walking out the store, a car full of guys pulled up. Joe immediately yelled out "Oh Shit"!

He then dropped the beer and started running. Larry yelled out for me to run, as he too started running.

I started running behind Joe and Larry not having any idea why.

We jumped fences, ran through back yards, and at the same time trying to avoid getting bit by dogs.

(Marco): Why are we running?

(Joe): Shut up, and run!

(Larry): Run as if your life depended on it!

Since I was a fast runner, and the fastest of them all, I ran pass Joe, and Larry and made it home before they did.

I was winded and tired. I never ran so fast in my life.

(Angel): What the hell is wrong? Where are Joe, and Larry?

(Marco): Right behind me.

(Angel): What the hell happen!?

(Marco): We were at the store, when Joe yelled out "Oh Shit", and ran. So Larry and I ran too.

At that point Joe and Larry finally made it back.

(Angel): What happen?

(Joe): Several guys from our number#1 rival gang showed up at the store.

(Angel): And you ran! You didn't stay to fight them!

(Larry): We had Marco with us.

(Joe): We know how you feel about him getting involved.

(Larry): We knew you'll get upset if he got hurt.

(Angel): Yeah, you guys are right. What the hell were they doing on our hood?

(Joe): Just showing disrespect.

(Angel): We'll take care of them another day.

(Larry): You just say the word.

(Angel): And the beer, what happen to the beer?

(Joe): I dropped it, and left it behind.

(Angel): They're probably enjoying our beer by now.

(Joe): Sorry

(Angel): Heck let's finish enjoying our party with what beer we have left.

It was then that I learned that the gang were having serious issues with a certain rival gang, and have become the worst of enemies, which had cause several violent rumbles between them already and have become the #1 rival gang.

This rival gang was the largest and meanest gang, and had been involved in many serious crimes. Many of their members had served time in prison, and several were still serving time.

We continued the party till about 1:00 a.m. Angel had everyone help clean up, before sending them home.

Angel and I were getting ready for bed and I was curious about what he meant by getting even with his #1 rival gang.

(Marco): What are you going to do about that other gang?

(Angel): Damn it! What did I tell you about asking questions involving the gang?

(Marco): Ok, ok, sorry.

(Angel): Just go to sleep, and don't worry about the gang. Don't even think about us.

(Marco): Ok, goodnight.

(Angel): Goodnight, Damn it!

I lay down by the window looking out, as Angel lay down next to me.

(Marco): Can I turn on the radio?

(Angel): Yeah, just keep it low.

(Marco): Ok, thanks.

Angel then grabbed my left hand and squeezed firmly.

(Angel): Hey.

(Marco): What?

(Angel): Sorry for shouting at you. Goodnight, love you.

(Marco): Love you too, but not as much as I love Sheryl.

(Angel): Auugh, you dork. You're wasting your time with her. See you in the morning.

(Marco): Ok, see in the morning.

(Marco): Hey.

(Angel): What now!

(Marco): She is really beautiful.

(Angel): Yeah, that she is.

(Marco): She must brag a lot about her looks?

(Angel): No she doesn't. She don't need to. She only shows it, now goodnight.

I listen to the radio and continued looking out the window until I fell asleep.

Another week had gone by, and again I spend it by doing around the house and helping neighbors with their needs. It was a Saturday afternoon, when Jacob showed up at the house looking for me.

(Jacob): Hey all the guys are going to the downtown plaza tonight, its Mo-Town night. You want to go?

(Marco): Na, you know that I am not allowed to hang with you guys.

(Jacob): Are you sure? Sheryl is going, and she asked me to invite you.

(Marco): What! Really! are you serious?

(Jacob): Yeah, she wants you there.

(Marco): Damn you Jacob don't joke with me.

(Jacob): I'm serious. Angel told me how hard you fell for her; this is your chance to be popular.

(Marco): Popular?

(Jacob): Kid, as beautiful as she is, you will be the talk of the hood, just by hanging around her. Heck, she will make you famous.

(Marco): Ha! She's not all that.

(Jacob): Ok, I'll tell her that you didn't want to come.

(Marco): No wait! What am I saying? Don't listen to me. She is all that and more. I'll be there.

(Jacob): Ok, see you there. Good luck.

I couldn't wait till Angel returned home from work. I would beg him to take me along with him. He finally arrived home. I ran up to the car, not giving him a chance to get off.

(Marco): You guys are going to the plaza tonight. I want to go. Take me with you.

(Angel): What? You're crazy. I don't want you around us.

(Marco): Angel please, Sheryl is going to be there, and she wants me to be there too.

A Moment in My Life

(Angel): She asked you to go?

(Marco): No, Jacob came by, and he told me.

(Angel): He's probably playing a joke on you, you dork.

(Marco): What? Are you guys playing with me?

(Angel): I'm not, but I'll take you, and if it's a joke, Jacob will pay for it.

(Marco): Wow! Thanks brother!

(Angel): And if it's true, you will only hang around with her, and not with the guys.

(Marco): Da! That's a no brainer.

(Angel): Must be those dimples?

(Marco): What?

(Angel): Like all the other girls, she must have fallen for your dimples.

(Marco): Oh well.

(Angel): Just kidding, she's going to like you. You're a great kid.

It took a lot of convincing, but mom and dad allowed me to go as long as Angel brought me back by midnight.

I was so excited. I took a quick shower and put on my dad's old spice cologne. I put on so much that it made me dizzy.

(Angel): Damn! You're going to wake up the dead with that much cologne on.

(Marco): Ok, I'm ready, let's go.

(Angel): Ok, don't be in such a hurry to have your heart broken.

(Marco): Ha! That will never happen.

(Angel): Ok, I warned you just prepare yourself.

Everyone was already there by the time we arrive, including Sheryl. She was looking great. Wow! She was a knockout.

Very nervously I started walking straight to her, hoping and praying that I would say the right words.

(Marco): Hi.

(Sheryl): Hey.

(Marco): We'll I'm here.

(Sheryl): Ok?

(Marco): Ok? Wait I'm here because of you.

(Sheryl): You are? Why?

(Marco): Well didn't you tell Jacob to invite me, because you wanted me to come.

(Sheryl): Ok maybe I did, and what is that smell?

(Marco): Oh, it's old spice.

(Sheryl): Well whatever it is, take it back to the car, and leave it there.

(Marco): It's cologne and it's on me.

(Sheryl): Did you showered in it?

(Marco): Too much huh?

(Sheryl): Well, I'll just hold my breath to keep from fainting.

(Marco): Wow! You'll faint over me? That would be cool.

(Sheryl): Shut-up. I didn't mean it as a compliment.

(Marco): Well, did you want me to be here?

(Sheryl): I guess, but don't ask me why.

(Marco): Maybe, because you like me?

(Sheryl): Or maybe because I'm only fourteen, and I don't know any better.

(Marco): No, it's because you like me.

(Sheryl): You're so full of it, and I don't mean of old spice.

(Marco): Gee's girl are you going to knock on me all night?

(Sheryl): Gee's boy, you're so sensitive.

(Marco): No I'm not. Look I just want to spend the time having fun with you, not you making fun of me.

(Sheryl): Do you think we can enjoy ourselves, and have fun together?

(Marco): Just give us a chance, and we'll be a hit. I promise.

At that point a song by the Chi-Lites (Write a letter to myself) started playing.

(Marco): We can start by dancing to this song.

(Sheryl): Ok, just stand against the wind.

(Marco): La' La' La'

(Sheryl): La' La' La' What?

(Marco): Never mind let's just dance.

We danced the entire song without saying a word to each other. God, she smelled so pretty.

(Marco): Thanks, that was a nice song.

(Sheryl): You like Mo-town music?

(Marco): Yeah, how about you.

(Sheryl): Yea, but my favorite group is Frankie Valli, and the Four Seasons.

(Marco): Really! They're my favorite group too. We now have something in common.

(Sheryl): Hey, the only thing we have in common is? Oh never mind. Let's dance to this song.

I couldn't believe the next song she wanted to dance to. It was (Stone in love with you) by the Stylistics that had started playing.

God, it felt great holding her close and tight while we dance.

(Marco): Hey, Angel says you're pretty enough to be an actress. I agree with him.

(Sheryl): Awww that was nice of him.

(Marco): Him, what about me? I agreed with him.

(Sheryl): Who listens to what you say? Stop talking, and just dance.

We didn't say another word for the rest of the song.

(Sheryl): Wow! that was a long song, let's go get a drink, I'm thirsty.

(Marco): Ok, I'm buying.

(Sheryl): You didn't expect me to buy, did you?

(Marco): La' La' La'

We walked over to the concession stand, bought some cold drinks, and talked.

(Sheryl): What are your plans for your future?

(Marco): I would like to become a cop.

(Sheryl): Are you serious, really?

(Marco): Yes I am.

(Sheryl): That's great.

(Marco): That's great? I was expecting for you to laugh at me.

(Sheryl): Of course not you silly. Never laugh at someone's dreams.

(My eyes adore you) by Frankie Valli started playing.

(Marco): Awww I love this song.

(Sheryl): That's our song, let's go dance.

(Marco): Hey! Wait a minute; you just said that's our song.

(Sheryl): Silly don't pay any attention to me, I'm only fourteen. Now shut up and let's go dance.

We danced, and we danced, and we danced, and we talked, and we joked, and we danced again until the end of the Festival.

I was right, we enjoyed the night, and we were a big hit.

The festival came to an end, and Angel walked over to us.

(Angel): Hey did you kids have fun?

(Marco): Yes, too bad the night is over.

(Angel): Good, you, Larry, and Pete escort the girls to the cars. I and the rest of the guys will catch up in a bit.

(Marco): What are you'll going to do?

(Angel): You dork. We met some girls, do I need to say more.

(Marco): Oh, Ok sorry.

Sheryl and I walked slowly behind the rest of the guys, as we walked through the parking lot.

(Sheryl): I had a lot of fun.

(Marco): Did you really?

She then bumped her shoulder against mine.

(Sheryl): Yes, I really did. Thank you.

(Marco): It was my pleasure.

(Sheryl): So you really want to be a cop.

(Marco): Yes, do you believe I can?

(Sheryl): Your chances will be greater if you stay away from the gang.

(Marco): They're my past; I'm no longer part of them.

(Sheryl):	That's great to hear, I wouldn't want you around me if your still part of them.
(Marco):	Are you saying that we are going to start hanging around together from here on?
(Sheryl):	I would like that very much.
(Marco):	Really?
(Sheryl):	Really, but I'm only fourteen……
(Marco):	I know, I know, you're only fourteen, don't listen to you.
(Sheryl):	Very good, you're catching on.
(Marco):	La' La' La'
(Sheryl):	Do you know the rest of the words to that song?
(Marco):	What song?
(Sheryl):	La' La' La' means I love you.
(Marco):	By the Del-fonics?
(Sheryl):	Yes, isn't that what you're trying to sing? You only say La' La' La.
(Marco):	Do you know the song?

(Sheryl): Yes it's a pretty song.

(Marco): Do you know what its saying?

(Sheryl): Of course I do, I know the English language.

(Marco): Auuuugh!

(Sheryl): I get you mad don't I?

(Marco): No you don't! You just like acting dumb.

(Sheryl): Well, I like acting dumb with you.

(Marco): Why are you so selfish?

(Sheryl): I haven't grown up yet, I'm only fourteen, and why are you so stubborn?

(Marco): Stubborn?

(Sheryl): Yes, the first time we met you were so stubborn; I couldn't get rid of you.

(Marco): Well, thanks to my stubbornness we are here today.

(Sheryl): Funny, but right.

We continued walking slowly, and having a good conversation, when all of a sudden we heard the girls screaming.

We looked up, and saw that Larry, and Pete were being assaulted by several guys, and the girls trying to get these guys off Larry and Pete.

(Marco):   Damn! You wait here!

I then ran to help Larry, and Pete.

(Sheryl):   What are you doing! Go get Angel!

I was then tackled to the ground from behind, and before I could throw the first punch, I had three guys on me. As I lay on the ground trying to avoid the kicks and punches I was receiving from these unknown guys, I could see Sheryl trying to get them off me.

One of the girls ran to get Angel, and the rest of the gang.

By the time Angel and the gang came to our rescue Larry, Pete, and I had already received a hell of a beating and the guys who did the beating had taken off in two different cars.

Angel picked me up off the ground.

(Angel):   Holy Shit! Are you ok?

(Marco):   Yes, I'm ok.

Angel then back handed me across the face.

(Angel): Damn you! What did I tell you! What hell did I tell you!

Everyone then shouted at Angel, telling him that it wasn't my fault. He paused for a minute, and then hugged me tight.

(Angel): I'm sorry, I love you, you stupid dork.

(Marco): Yeah? You sure have a funny way of showing it.

(Angel): Larry, Pete who were they?

(Larry): They were our number 1 rival gang.

(Angel): Are you sure?

(Pete): Yeah, that's who they were, we're sure.

(Angel): Are you guys ok.

(Larry): Yea.

(Pete): Yea, I'm ok.

(Angel): You girls go home; the rest of us will meet at the pool hall in an hour.

(Sheryl): Marco, are you sure you're ok?

(Marco): Yes, I'm ok.

(Sheryl): Here's my number, call me.

(Marco): Ok, I will.

She hugged and thanked me for the night. That sure made the pain go away.

(Sheryl): Talk to you later.

(Marco): Ok, I really had a wonderful time.

(Sheryl): I'm not kidding. I really did too.

(Angel): Well you two dummies just shut-up already.

We heard police sirens getting closer, so we hurried to ours cars. Angel and I headed for home.

We didn't say a word to each other until we arrived home.

(Angel): Go in through the back door, and straight to bed. I'll be back later.

(Marco): What are you guys going to do?

(Angel): Do as I say, and don't asked questions. Now get out of the car.

(Marco): Ok, see you later. Be careful.

I started getting out of the car when Angel grabbed my arm.

(Angel): Hey dork, I'll be ok little brother.

(Marco): Just get home safe.

Angel drove off, and I went straight to bed, but I was unable to go to sleep, just worried and wondering what Angel's plans were to get even with the other gang.

It was around four in the morning when Angel finally return home. He turned on the bedroom light, and I immediately notice that he was bleeding from the upper right eye, and the mouth.

(Marco): Are you ok? What happen?

(Angel): I'm doing fine, don't ask questions.

(Marco): How about the rest of the guys?

(Angel): They're all ok. Now go to sleep.

Angel went to the rest room to treat his wounds, and then came and lay next to me.

(Angel): We kicked butt. Goodnight dork.

(Marco): Goodnight.

A Moment in My Life

I turned on the radio, and just stared out the window, happy to see that Angel returned home safe, and of course thinking of my time with Sheryl. I couldn't wait to see her again.

It was when I call Sheryl the next day that I learned that Angel and the gang went into the other gang territory, and rumble with them.

According to Sheryl, some of the guys ended up in jail, and others ended up in the hospital. Within a week everybody was out of jail and the hospital.

(Sheryl): Enough talk about those dummies, do you want to go skating tonight?

(Marco): Yea! I would love to.

(Sheryl): Great, Sharon, and I will pick you up around 7:00 O'clock. Is that ok with you?

(Marco): Yes, but couldn't you make it sooner? I like to spend more time with you.

(Sheryl): I would like to, but Sharon won't have the car till then.

(Marco): Ok, I guess it would be worth the wait.

(Sheryl): Of course, you're going with me.

(Marco): Blah, Blah, Blah

(Sheryl): I really get you mad don't I?

(Marco): La' La' La'

(Sheryl): I La' La' La' you too.

(Marco): What! Really!

(Sheryl): I don't know. I'm only fourteen. Well, I'll see you tonight, bye.

(Marco): Ok, bye.

I hurried to the bedroom. Angel was still asleep.

(Marco): Angel wake up, wake up.

(Angel): Dang it you dork, what is it?

(Marco): I'm going skating with Sheryl tonight.

(Angel): So what do you want my blessing?

(Marco): No, I need money, can I borrow five dollars?

Angel sat up, and asked me to sit next to him.

(Angel): You're really into her, huh?

(Marco): Yeah, I like her a lot.

(Angel): She's a heart breaker, and she has already broken a lot of hearts for her age.

(Marco): You can hold my heart.

(Angel): What?

(Marco): Yeah, you see, if you hold my heart, she wouldn't have a chance to break it.

(Angel): You're such a dork! Take the money from my wallet, and enjoy yourselves. I'm going back to sleep.

(Marco): Thanks.

(Angel): Yeah, yeah what a dork.

Instead of five I took seven dollars, and hurried to the shower. I then changed into some of my good clothes, and splashed some Old Spice Cologne on me, but just a little bit this time.

I went and sat in the living room couch and waited for Sheryl, when I notice the clock showing that it was only 5:00 O'clock.

Mom and the rest of the kids were already in the living room watching The Three Stooges. They were one of our favorite shows.

(Mom): Ok, why are you looking, and smelling so pretty?

(Marco): Pretty? Mom pretty is for girls.

(Mom): You know what I mean, where are you going, and with who?

(Marco): Sheryl invited me to go skating with her.

(Mom): That was very nice of her. Whose taking you'll?

(Marco): Sheryl sister Sheron.

(Mom): What time are they picking you up?

(Marco): 7:00 O'clock.

(Mom): You still have two hours.

(Marco): I know, I guess I'll just sit here, and watch T.V. with you'll.

(Mom): Oh, like a family moment?

Like a family moment, we hadn't had one of those in many years. I had forgotten what that was like.

You see once a week, usually on a Friday night mom, and dad would gather all the kids in the living room to watch a movie, usually a Project Terror

Movie, and we all shared a large bowl of popcorn while watching the movie.

After the movie was over, Dad would tell us creepy stories, such as the crying lady in the lake, or the owl with the lady face. After the stories we were sent straight to bed.

Yes those were times I enjoyed, because I always sat next to Angel, and he would always placed his arm around me, as to tell me not to worry about the lady or the owl, he would take care of me.

That all stopped when Angel and I became too old to take part in our family moments. So we thought.

So I sat in the living room watching T.V. with the family, until they finally arrived to pick me up. It was 20 minutes till 7:00.

(Marco): Have to go mom, love you.

(Mom): Ok, enjoy yourselves.

I hurried out to the car, and saw that Sheryl was standing outside the car holding the back door open for me.

(Marco): You don't have to do this for me.

(Sheryl): You keep forgetting, that am only fourteen, and I don't know any better.

(Marco): Well, how long before you turn fifteen?

(Sheryl): In two months.

I hopped into the back seat, and Sheryl closed the door behind, as she hopped back into the front seat. I was surprise she didn't seat with me. Sheryl then leaned over the front seat.

(Sheryl): Well, aren't going to ask me why I'm not sitting back there with you.

(Marco): I already know.

(Sheryl): You do?

(Marco): Yeah, you're only fourteen, and you don't know why you do these stupid things.

Sharon then started laughing as we drove off.

(Sharon): Tuto that was funny.

(Sheryl): Don't call him that! Call him by his real name!

(Sharon): Ok, ok, don't get upset. I'm just use to calling him Tuto.

I haven't heard the name Tuto in a long while.

(Sheryl):   That is history, his past.

Sheryl then looked me straight in the eye.

(Sheryl):   Isn't that right Marco?

(Marco):   Yeah, that's right Sharon. Don't call me Tuto anymore.

(Sharon):   AAyyy por favor, "Sir "whatever you say.

Sheryl grabbed an eight track tape of Frankie Valli, and the Four Seasons, and started playing it. We listen to it until we arrived at the skating ring.

The rest of the girls from the gang were there, but none of the guys, and according to Sharon they had other plans, and they weren't showing up.

That only made me wondered what they were up to, and if Angel was part of it. But I didn't dare ask and I didn't want to know.

Sheryl and I were having a lot of fun skating, laughing, and just making fun of others who were falling on their butts. It was the first time we held hands.

It was from that night on that we became in separable. We just couldn't stand to be apart from each other. We even wrote letters to ourselves and pretended it came from the other. We would then exchange them with each other and read what each other had written, and then laugh about it. It was nothing but laughs, laughs, and laughs, when we were together, and there was not a worry in the world for us. Sheryl also made sure that I stayed away from the gang.

We enjoyed ourselves by going to the movies, skating, hanging around the city park, or downtown or just listen to some records at her home. We just had something to do every day.

The skating ring was getting ready to close for the night, so we went to a close by hamburger joint. We listen to songs from the music box as we sat next to each other eating our burgers, and sharing the fries.

(Sheryl): Hey, a friend of mine is having her fifteen birthday debut, and she asked me to stand in it.

(Marco): Oh yeah, when?

(Sheryl): In three weeks, it's on a Saturday.

(Marco): Who's standing with you?

(Sheryl): No one if you don't go.

A Moment in My Life

(Marco): You mean you want me to stand with you?

(Sheryl): Aaahhh here we go again.

(Marco): I know, I know, you're only fourteen, and you don't know why…………

(Sheryl): No Marco, stop asking me if I'm sure about things I want.

(Marco): I'm I doing that?

(Sheryl): Kind of sort of, yes.

(Marco): I'm sorry, but yes I'll stand in the debut with you.

(Sheryl): Great and you only have three weeks to get a tuxedo.

(Marco): I'll go get one tomorrow.

(Sheryl): And there is something else we have to do before the debut.

(Marco): What? I'll do anything.

(Sheryl): We'll have to go to church and confess our sins.

(Marco): Wow, that's going to take the whole day for me.

(Sheryl): Seriously Marco.

(Marco): No, just kidding, of course I'll do it.

    It was getting late, and Sharon asked us to hurry up and finish our burgers. We did, and headed for home. This time Sheryl sat in the back seat with me, and talked about the debut.

    We finally made to my house, and I thanked Sharon for taking us.

(Sheryl): I had a lot of fun.

(Marco): Did you?

(Sheryl): Of course. I'm only fourteen; kids our age are supposed to be enjoying life.

(Marco): God help me! I give up.

(Sheryl): Hey!

(Marco): What!

(Sheryl): Don't forget the debut in three weeks!

(Marco): I won't!

(Sheryl): Hey!

(Marco): Now what!

A Moment in My Life

(Sheryl): La' La' La'

(Marco): Dang you Sheryl, you're driving me crazy.

(Sheryl): Goodnight, I'll talk to you later, and stop being so sensitive.

(Marco): Goodnight, thanks for the time, I enjoyed it very much.

I hurried straight to the bedroom. Angel was in there shinning his shoes.

(Angel): Well, did you have fun?

(Marco): Of course I did, and she asked me to stand in a debut with her.

(Angel): She did?

(Marco): Yes!

(Angel): She must really like you.

(Marco): There's only one problem. I need a tuxedo, and I don't have any money for it.

(Angel): This means a lot to you?

(Marco): Yeah, and I know we are both very young, but it's all about fun and laughs, and feeling great around each other.

(Angel): Well, I see nothing wrong with that. The tuxedo is on me.

(Marco): Wow, thanks a lot. I knew I could count on you. Can we go get it tomorrow?

(Angel): Yes, I'll take you tomorrow.

(Marco): Great, I'm going to get ready for bed. I can't wait till tomorrow. Goodnight.

(Angel): Hey, before you go to sleep, I need to tell you something.

(Marco): What is it?

(Angel): Sharon told me that Sheryl really felt hard for you.

(Marco): Really!

(Angel): Yea, but you are right. You are both very young, and need to concentrate on your future and nothing else. Sharon feels the same way too.

(Marco): Are you and Sharon going to try and keep us apart?

(Angel): God you're such a dork! No, we just want you both not to forget your plans for both your futures.

(Marco): Ok, I promise. Goodnight.

Morning couldn't come soon enough. Angel and I headed to the closes tuxedo place, and I was measure for one. I loved the way I looked in it.

(Marco): Do I look ok in it?

(Angel): Yes you do. You're going to break some hearts.

I walked over to Angel hugged him and thanked him for the tuxedo and walked back to the mirror.

(Angel): Now what's wrong?

(Marco): I don't have any shoes to go with the tuxedo.

(Angel): Well as soon as we are finish here we are going to a shoe store.

(Marco): Wow, thanks Angel.

(Angel): Hey, these are not all free.

(Marco): What do you mean?

(Angel): You're going to pay it all back, when you because rich and famous.

(Marco): Rich and famous?

(Angel): Well, when you become someone earning good money.

(Marco): Ok.

We finish at the tuxedo store, and headed for the shoe store. We spend half the day together enjoying each other company, and Angel giving me lectures about the importance of an education. I didn't mind, as long as I was just enjoying my time with him.

Another week went by, Sheryl and I spend it hanging around together, mostly at her house watching T.V., or playing records. Saturday night came and Angel invited me to go with him and some of guys to the drive-in.

Angel had some of the guys hide in the trunk of the car as he paid at the entrance. The movie was of King Kong versus Godzilla. It was a very boring movie. So we played a dare game which I ended up being the looser.

The looser was to run only in his underwear across the parking lot. Not being one to back down from a dare, I did just that, and was chased out of the drive-in, in my underwear's by some Deputy Constables who were providing security there.

A Moment in My Life

I was picked up a block down from the drive-in by Angel and the guys who were holding my clothes and laughing very hard.

(Angel): You're such a dork. Get in the car before an old man see's you and wants to take you home with him.

(Marco): Hey I won the dare game didn't I?

(Angel): Auuugh!! No you dork. You lost, that's why you are running around like a fool in your underwear's.

(Marco): But I took the dare.

Cause you lost! Everyone shouted at the same time.

We then dropped off the guys at their homes, and we headed home ourselves.

Sheryl heard I of the dare game, and wasn't too happy about it. But she didn't stay mad too long. She forgave me and told me to grow up and not do it again.

The time came for us to show up at the church to confess our sins three days before the day of the debut.

Everyone who was to stand on the debut showed up and took turns walking into the confession box. I guess that's what they call it? I didn't know too much about church.

My turn came, so I went into the confession box, and started telling the priest about all the wrongs I have done. I was very surprise, when the priest walked out of his box, and walked over to my box, then took me out, and escorted me out of the church.

(Marco):   What happen? What Did I do wrong?

(Priest):   You will be welcome back, when you learn to conduct yourself in a proper manor.

The priest closed the door on me, and I remember staring at the door saying to myself. "What the hell just happen here?"

(Sheryl):   Marco what happen? What did you do?

(Marco):   I have no idea. I confessed to everything I did wrong, and asked for forgiveness and the next thing I know is I'm standing outside the church.

(Sheryl):   Did you confess to being the devil himself?

Sheryl appeared to be upset and embarrass. I was confused. We didn't feel like hanging around with the others, so we took the bus home. We didn't say a word to each other through the entire bus ride.

I walked Sheryl home from where the bus dropped us off, and still not saying a word to each other. We finally made it to her house.

(Marco): I'll talk to you later.

(Sheryl): You want to come in for a soda?

(Marco): Na, I better get home.

(Sheryl): No, I'm sorry, but we are not going to end the day like this. You are going to come in have a soda with me and talk about this.

So I did as Sheryl asked and by the end of the day we were both laughing about the entire incident.

As for the priest, well many years later he became the Arch Bishop, and still assigned to stay in the city.

Several days later Sheryl called me with some bad news. You see the parents of the girls having the debut were very religious, and because of what happen with me at the church I was not going to be allowed to stand with Sheryl at the debut.

(Sheryl): I don't think it's fair so I'm not going either.

(Marco): This is the time not to act like you're only fourteen. We are talking about your friend's debut.

(Sheryl): I don't want to go without you.

(Marco): You can't let your friend down. You have to go.

(Sheryl): Are you sure?

(Marco): Yes, I'm very sure of it.

(Sheryl): You know that I'm going to have to ask someone else to stand with me.

(Marco): Yeah, I figured that already, and I know you're not going to have any problem getting someone right away.

(Sheryl): Hey, why don't you show up for the dance?

(Marco): Na, I'm sure your friends parents won't want be there.

(Sheryl): Damn you Marco, nothing was supposed to get in between us.

(Marco): Look I have to go. I'll talk to you later. Have fun.

(Sheryl): Oh don't worry; I will have lots of fun. Bye!

Three days later the day of the debut came, and I hadn't spoken to Sheryl in those three days.

I was in the bedroom lying on the bed staring at the tuxedo hanging on the wall and looking at the clock. 6:00 O'clock came around and I started to picture Sheryl walking down the aisle with her arm around another guys arm. I could feel tears wanting to run down my cheeks, but I held myself together and tried to force myself to go to sleep.

It was at that point that Angel walked into the room wearing a suit.

(Marco): Why are you wearing a suit? Where are you going?

(Angel): I was hired to be a chauffeur today.

(Marco): You got a job as a chauffeur? How much does that pay?

(Angel): Marco you're still such a dork. I'm your chauffeur!

(Marco): My chauffeur? What are you talking about?

Mom then walked into the room with a smile.

(Mom): There's a pretty young lady in the living room wanting to talk to you.

(Marco): Who?

(Angel): Probably the same person who hired me.

(Marco): ?????

I then walked into the living room and was surprise to see Sheryl sitting on the couch wearing the dress she was to wear at the debut.

(Marco): Sheryl?

(Sheryl): I rather let my friend down and not you.

(Mom): Well aren't you going to tell her how beautiful she looks.

(Marco): You really do.

(Sheryl): Are you going to put on your tuxedo?

(Marco): Yea! Give me five minutes. Where are we going?

(Angel): Just hurry up! I want to get out of this monkey suit.

Sheryl didn't hire Angel to chauffer us around. She only asked him if he would. Not only was he happy to do it, but he paid for everything.

First he took us to a fancy restaurant, and then he took us to a movie theater, and after that he drove us around downtown. We were having a hell of a wonderful time.

(Sheryl): Is it that time yet?

(Angel): Yeah, it's that time.

(Marco): Time for what? It's still early.

(Angel): You dork the date is not over yet. There's another place I have to take you.

(Marco): Where?

(Sheryl): Don't ask. It's a surprise.

Angel drove us to Sheryl house.

(Marco): You said the date wasn't over. Why are we here?

(Angel): It's a surprise from Sheryl and the gang.

(Sheryl): Come on; walk with me to the back yard.

What the gang had done was fix up the back yard to look like a dance hall, and it was all Sheryl's idea.

The entire gang was there and all we did for the remainder of the night was dance and listen to several of our favorite songs.

(Marco): You guys did all these for me.

(Sheryl): It was my idea, and I did it for us.

(Marco): Thank you, it means a lot to me.

It was one of the best times I have ever had, and Sheryl was responsible to for it.

It was around 2:00 O'clock in the morning when we decided to shut down the party. I thanked the gang and Sheryl for everything.

(Sheryl): I'm glad it turned out just the way I wanted it.

(Marco): La' La' La'

(Sheryl): Why don't you just say it?

(Marco): Say what?

(Sheryl): I love you, instead of just La' La' La'.

(Marco): Do you really want me to tell you that?

A Moment in My Life

(Sheryl): Auuugh Marco! Never mind, La' La' La' is good enough.

(Sheryl): La' La' La' back to you.

(Angel): Are you two retarded? Come on dork, let's head for home.

(Marco): I'll call you tomorrow.

(Sheryl): Ok, maybe we can do something tomorrow?

(Marco): Ok.

(Angel): Gee's, don't you two see enough of each other?

Angel and I went home and straight to bed, and as usual I turned on the radio and stared out the window thinking of Sheryl until I felt asleep.

Angel woke me up around 11:00 O'clock.

(Angel): Hey, get up. Let's go fishing.

(Marco): Really! ok.

I called Sheryl and told her what I was going to do, and she understood as long as it was only Angel and not the rest of the gang.

Angel decided to walk to the lake, and even though it was going to be a long walk I didn't mind because it was going to give us more time together.

We had already walked about two miles when Angel decided to visit a friend at a house we happen to walk by. He had me wait outside by the street curb.

So I waited and started tossing rocks across the street. About thirty minutes had gone by when a car pulled up to the house and a man exit the car and walked into the same house.

Maybe that's Angel's friend I wondered. Seconds later I see Angel climbing out the side window and running toward me.

(Angel): Run!!!

(Marco): What! Why!

(Angel): Just run dork!!!

I ran as fast as I could, I was two steps ahead of Angel. I left the fishing poles and our lunch box behind.

(Marco): Why are we running!!

(Angel): That was my friends' husband who showed up! Just keep running!

A Moment in My Life

So we ran until we couldn't run anymore.

(Marco): Angel you are crazy.

(Angel): Hey where's our lunch box?

(Marco): I left it behind.

(Angel): And our fishing poles?

(Marco): Left them behind too.

(Angel): You dork, why do I bring you with me?

(Marco): So you can have someone to talk too?

(Angel): Yea, I guess, but you're still a dork.

We continued walking until we finally made it to the lake. We sat at Angel's favorite spot. We didn't enjoy fishing, but it was Angel's excuse to get away from the hood, and he always dragged me along with him.

We sat around for awhile and started talking. It was mostly about my future.

(Angel): So have you thought of what you want to do with your life?

(Marco): What would you say if I said I want to be a cop?

(Angel): You can do better than that.

(Marco): How's that?

(Angel): You can become a police officer.

(Marco): I just said that.

(Angel): No, you said you want to become a cop.

(Marco): What is the difference?

(Angel): You know that cop that we know to be short tempered, and heavy handed?

(Marco): Yea, he's a bad cop.

(Angel): That's right, and he will always be just that "a cop". But a police officer is not in it for himself. Not only will he enforce the laws, but he will abide by them too. He will police himself and respect the rights of others.

(Marco): Oh, I see what you mean.

(Angel): So a police officer is what you want to be?

(Marco): Yea, that's my dream.

(Angel): Well, you will never become one.

(Marco): What? Why?

A Moment in My Life

(Angel): You know that King guy.

(Marco): Elvis?

(Angel): Auuugh!! You're such a dork! I mean that black guy that was going around saying he had a dream, before he was killed.

(Marco): Oh yea, what about him?

(Angel): Well that was his problem. He and others like him who only dreams for a future instead of planning for it. I don't want you to dream for yours. You have to plan for it.

(Marco): I understand. It makes sense.

We stayed quiet for about ten minutes.

(Marco): Hey, Benny always used to say to me "Don't just be Recognized, be notice". What was he trying to tell me?

(Angel): You see that group of guys standing over by the bridge.

(Marco): Yea, what about them?

(Angel): Well, what do you notice about that group?

(Marco): There's a guy way taller than the others?

(Angel): Right, so you notice him as the tallest of the group. You see when you become a police officer you will only be recognize as being a part of the force, until you do something spectacular then you will be notice, and you will stand out.

(Marco): You said when I become a police officer, not if?

(Angel): What you have doubts, cause I don't.

If you say you want to be one, then you will be one. I believe in you.

(Marco): What about you and your future?

(Angel): It's too late for me.

(Marco): What do you mean?

(Angel): No one will ever give me a chance. I have a damage reputation.

(Marco): You've always talked about opening your own mechanic business.

(Angel): That's takes a lot of money that I will never see in my life, and there's no one that will take a chance on me.

(Marco): Have you given up?

(Angel): I'm just concentrating on your future right now.

We continued talking and even took a short nap. Angel woke up first, and then he woke me up.

(Angel): Come on it's getting late, and thanks to you I'm hungry. Let's head for home.

(Marco): Yea, I'm very hungry myself.

We gather ourselves together and starting the long journey back home.

It was very hot, and we had already walked about three miles, when Angel notice a police officer parked at a store parking lot.

(Angel): There's a police officer, come on let's go ask him for a favor.

(Marco): A favor?

(Angel): Don't say anything; let me do all the talking.

Angel told the officer that we had broken down and had walked the last three miles, and that we needed to get home soon, because I needed my medication for my seizures. The officer was nice enough to take us home.

(Angel): Officer my little dork brother wants to become a police officer too. Do you have any advice for him?

(Officer): Finish school, and stay out of trouble.

(Angel): And tell him to stop being a dork.

(Officer): That would help.

We made it home, and we thanked the officer for his assistance

(Officer): Hope to see you in the force one of these years.

(Marco): Thanks. Bye.

(Angel): Again thanks for your help, and stay safe.

(Angel): You see, now his a police officer.

(Marco): Yea, I see what you mean.

I hurried inside the house and called Sheryl. I told her about how the fishing trip went.

(Sheryl): Did Angel talk to you about having a party for your birthday?

(Marco): No he didn't. But my birthday was two weeks ago, I thought he had forgotten?

(Sheryl): Well he didn't forget, and he made plans to have the party here at my house.

(Marco): Really?

(Sheryl): I'm surprise he didn't tell you.

(Marco): Maybe it was suppose to be a surprise, and you should not have told me.

(Sheryl): Oh shit! What if you're right?

(Marco): I think you just ruin the surprise.

(Sheryl): Oh my god, I think you are right. Oh well I'm only fourteen, and I don't know any better.

Sheryl invited me to come over to the house, and listen to some records, and I ran over to her house as quickly as I could. We had a great time, just acting silly and having lots of laughs. We just didn't want this great time that we were having come to an end. But it was getting close to midnight, and I called Angel to pick me up. Sheryl and I made plans to hang around downtown the following day, and said our goodnights.

(Marco): Hey Sheryl told me about the party you have planned for me.

(Angel): What! It was suppose to be a surprise. She's a dork too.

(Marco): You have to forgive her. She's only fourteen.

(Angel): She's still a dork, maybe you two dorks do belong together.

(Marco): Yeah, maybe we do right?

(Angel): You just concentrate on your future. Don't let her or anything else interfering with your future, and I don't want you to interfere with hers.

(Marco): Ok, I know, but her future is with me.

(Angel): Only if it is meant to be.

(Marco): Believe me, it is meant to be. She just doesn't know it yet.

   I stayed quiet for awhile just thinking.

(Angel): What's wrong? What are you thinking about?

(Marco): What if things don't work out for us.

(Angel): Again whatever happens, it's because it was meant to be.

(Marco): I guess.

(Angel): Look little brother you need to understand that there is nothing permanent in life except death. The sooner you understand this, the easier life will be.

(Marco): Yeah, I guess. Hey thanks for remembering my birthday.

(Angel): How could I forget, now you're a sixteen year old dork?

(Marco): You like calling me dork?

(Angel): With a lot of love little brother, with a lot of love.

We made it home. I went to mom's room, and sat next to her as she laid there sleeping. She woke up, and we talked about my future, and about Angel. Oh, and a little bit about Sheryl.

It was getting close to 2:00 O'clock in the morning. Mom wanted to go back to sleep, and I was getting sleepy myself. We said our goodnights, I went to my bedroom, and quickly fell asleep.

Sheryl and I spend the rest of the week together. We hung around downtown just window shopping, we went swimming, horseback riding, the zoo and the amusement park.

I remember one time at one of her acting lessons she role played a very sad scene. She was so good and convincing and she made it look so real that I almost cried. We just had a wonderful week having lots of fun with each other.

I remember both Sheryl and I telling each other how we wish that there were more hours in a day, and more days in a week.

It was a Friday evening the day before my birthday party. I was at Sheryl's house. I was playing records and she was role playing some scenes from movies that I would choose for her to act to.

She would role played all the characters from the Wizard of Oz movie, Ellie Mae from the Beverly Hills Billie's show, and other actors like John Wayne, Charlie Chaplin.

(Marco): You're good, you should be an actress.

(Sheryl): Maybe I will.

(Marco): Blah, Blah, Blah

(Sheryl): I just hope that whatever future we dream of comes true.

(Marco): Then don't dream of a future. You need to plan for it.

(Sheryl): What?

(Marco): Just something Angel said. He said that we need to plan for our future, not dream for them.

(Sheryl): Well, that makes sense.

Sheryl then started putting on some high heels shoes.

(Marco): What are you doing?

(Sheryl): Put on that song by Billy Williams. I want to tap dance to that song for you.

(Marco): Which song?

(Sheryl): Write a letter to myself.

She tapped dance half the song, and she was so funning doing it. This girl has everything that makes me happy. I remembered thinking to myself.

It was getting late, and I decided not to call Angel to pick me up. I walked home, and called Sheryl as soon as I made it home, just to let her know that I made it safe.

(Sheryl): Ok, get enough sleep, because tomorrow is the party.

(Marco): Yeah, I can't wait.

(Sheryl): Hey.

(Marco): What?

(Sheryl): La' La' La', goodnight.

(Marco): Yeah, me too, goodnight.

The day of my party came. Angel called me to tell me that he was getting off work late, and he would see me at Sheryl house.

I put on my best clothes and showed up at Sheryl house around 7:00 O'clock. Everybody was there and Sheryl was looking so beautiful as always.

It was already going on an hour and Angel still hadn't showed up. We decided to cut the cake, which I hesitantly did because it was Angel who bought the cake and I wanted him to be there when I did.

It was going on 9:30, and Angel still hadn't shown up, so I decided to call home.

Janie my older sister answered the phone and immediately I could tell something was wrong because she was crying. She told me that mom and dad went to the hospital because something serious had happen to Angel.

I had Sharon drive me to the hospital emergency room, where I met mom and dad. Mom was crying.

(Mom): They almost killed him.

(Marco): Who? What happen?

(Dad): Police officer said Angel was stabbed by some guys from a gang.

(Marco): How bad is it?

(Mom): He made not make it.

(Marco): Can I see him?

(Dad): Not right now, the doctors are still operating on him.

We waited for about an hour before we were allowed to see him. We couldn't believe what we were seeing. He had tubes coming out of his mouth and nose. We all just hugged each other and cried.

I was hurting so much for Angel, but I also had a strong feeling of anger in me, something I have never experience before in my life.

Angel pulled through, and I visited with him every day. The day he was able to talk he told me that he went shopping for my birthday gift, when he was attack by several guys from the number 1 rival gang, and they took the watch he had bought me for my birthday.

I still had so much anger in me, and I promise Angel I would get even. He tried to tell me to stay out of it; but I just wouldn't listen to him this time. Those bastards almost took him away from me.

The following day I gathered all the guys together and told them of what I had learned from Angel, and I wasn't going to let the other gang get away with it.

Knowing that Angel was going to get very upset with the guys, they decided to stand with me anyway. We all drove to a pool hall in the other gang's territory where several of them were. We tore up the place, and gave them a hell of a beating. I had so much anger that I was forcibly pulled off the guy I was beating on. Once again I was part of the gang and I had broken my promise to Angel and my parents. But I had mix emotions about it.

I went to go visit Sheryl the next day. She was hurt and very upset.

(Sheryl): You idiot, why did go rumble with the gang.

(Marco): I just felt that I needed to get even for Angel.

(Sheryl): You're going to end up like him, or even worst.

(Marco): I did what I had to do.

(Sheryl): Well, this is it for us.

(Marco): What? What are you saying?

(Sheryl): You're part of the gang again. I don't want you around me.

(Marco): You're only fourteen. You don't know what you're saying.

(Sheryl): I'm nothing joking Marco, or should I call you Tuto?

(Marco): Come on Sheryl, you're not serious.

(Sheryl): You disappointed me. Good luck on your future.

Sheryl was true to her word. She asked me to leave, and never to call her or come by again. And just like that it was over. As quickly as she came into my life, she was out just as fast. That was the last time we spoke.

I didn't give up on her that easy. I did show up at her house several times, asking her to come out, and talk to me, but with no success. I even called her several times hoping that she would talk to me, and again with no success. Yep, it was the last time we spoke to each other.

Years later after high school, she married, and moved to another state. Even though in my mind I wished her the best, it was my heart saying that she had married the wrong guy.

Have I wondered what would have become of us if I hadn't rejoined the gang again? Yes, of course I have. Up to this day I still do. I have driven by her old house many times, and all I see are beautiful memories.

Angel stayed in the hospital for four weeks before he was release. He just stayed at home for another three weeks healing, by that time we had already violently rumble with the #1 rival gang a total of four times without him.

Angel wasn't too happy with me, but he knew that I was already in it too deep, and he knew he needed to protect me, even if it meant me continuing to rumble along side with the gang.

Angel was finally ready to join us, and realizing that our #1 rival gang were too large of a gang he recruited gang members from other gangs to fight along with us.

The rumbles were getting more violent than ever before. We were no longer avoiding each other. We were now out looking for each other, and we were rumbling all over the city, where ever we ran into each other. If the guys weren't ending up in jail, they were ending up in the hospital. School registration came, and I fell to registered. Mom and dad had become very upset and disappointed with me.

It finally came. The night Angel decided to get all this over with, once and for all. He had made plans to crash a wedding party, where every member of our #1 rival gang were going to be at.

It was around 11:00 O'clock at night. We all went in seven different vehicles. Of course I was in the same car with Angel; he would never leave me out of his site.

(Angel): This is it little brother, the rumble that will end all rumbles. Win or lose.

(Marco): Really? Can we stop this already?

(Angel): You're tired of this shit too?

(Marco): Yea, I am. I don't want to rumble anymore.

(Angel): Good, that's what I want to hear.

We arrived at the wedding place, it was being held outside. I could see the bride enjoying her moment, and we were about to ruin it.

What made it easy for both me and Angel was the fact that the groom was one of the #1 rival gang leaders and one of the guys that stabbed Angel almost killing him.

Angel finally gave the signal, and we crashed the wedding. Tables, chairs and bottles were flying across the room. I could hear women and children screaming and crying, an innocent people getting hurt.

A Moment in My Life

All of a sudden I couldn't stand to see or hear anymore. I ran up to the bride and shouted to her that I was very sorry. I continued running, and I ran, and ran until I made to the highway.

I then started to hitch hiked and I have no idea how I did it, but I made it to a little town named Coolidge in Arizona.

I came across an Arizona Trooper, I told him who I was, and I wanted to get back home.

Arrangements were made and I was sent back home on a Grey Hound Bus. Dad was waiting for me when I arrived. I hopped into the car, and immediately notice all my clothes in the back seat.

(Marco): Why are all my clothes in the back seat?

(Dad): You're going to go live somewhere else. It's not too late for you.

(Marco): Does mom know about this?

(Dad): It was both our ideas.

Not another word was said. Dad rented me a one room apartment far away from the hood and paid for two months in advance. The landlord was an elderly lady, and she promise dad that she would make sure I had everything I needed.

And just like that I was on my own. I remember crying every night for the first three nights. I was feeling abandoned and unwanted, just thinking if what mom and dad were doing to me was even legal.

Angel went out of his way to stay away from me. He would even stay away from home every time I stopped by to visit with the family. I never saw, or spoke to him again, at least for the next twenty five years.

But something good came out of all this. By Mom and dad moving me out of the house and Angel avoiding me, it made me understand the meaning of unconditional love. It also made me understand what responsibility was all about?

To support myself I lied about my age to get a job as a custodian at a nursing home. I enrolled at a local community college, and earn my General Equivalent Diploma.

I then continued my studies and applied for a position with the County Sheriff's Dept.

A Moment in My Life

I was hired in 1980, and that was the beginning of my wonderful career in Law Enforcement.

As for Angel, well he continued going in and out of jail, until he was finally sentences to serve time in state prison. I never did write to him or visit with him, it was his wish. Up to this day I have never learned why he was sentence, nor do I wish to ever know.

I had already been in Law-Enforcement for over twenty years, when Angel was finally release from prison.

I was finally going to get to see him for the first time in over twenty years, and I was very excited.

I was in uniform when I went to go see him at mom's house. We hugged and cried, and he thanked me for making something of my life.

He also reminded me that I was still a dork.

But his release was bitter sweet. He had been diagnosed with cancer and didn't have much longer to live. I remember thinking to myself that he was going to leave me once again. This time was forever.

He did not lived more than 8 months after his release and I spent every single available minute with him until his last day. I made every minute count.

I would take him back to his favorite spot at the lake, and all we did was reminisce about our childhood and teenage years. We didn't leave the summer of 1974 out of our conversation either. I guess it was because that was the beginning of my future and the end of his.

I also remember asking him if he was scare of dying. He said dying was easy; it was living that was hard for him. The day before he passed away he promises me that he would do better next time. That only made me wondered if he believed in reincarnation. And if there's any truth to reincarnation, then it would be wonderful to run alongside of him once again.

We had his body cremated. His ashes are at home with me, next to all the awards, ribbons, and medals I have earned as a Law Enforcement Officer.

It's been over thirty years, and I still continue to think of Sheryl, especially when I hear the songs that we use to dance, and listen to. I strongly believe that I will always have her memories with me for the rest of my life, and I hope that before my life is over, I would once again run into this beautiful person, and just say to her thank you, and it was for real.

A Moment in My Life

As for Angel, do I miss him? Yes every day.

Do I think of him? Every time I put on the uniform.

Cheers to you big brother, from your brother the dork ☺.

CPSIA information can be obtained at www.ICGtesting.com
Printed in the USA
BVOW08*0618240216

437872BV00002B/65/P